Instructions to a son, containing rules of conduct in publick and private life, ... By Archibald Marquis of Argyle. ... To which are added ... general maxims of life. ...

Archibald Campbell

ECCO

PRINT EDITIONS

Eighteenth Century
Collections Online
Print Editions

Gale ECCO Print Editions

Relive history with *Eighteenth Century Collections Online*, now available in print for the independent historian and collector. This series includes the most significant English-language and foreign-language works printed in Great Britain during the eighteenth century, and is organized in seven different subject areas including literature and language; medicine, science, and technology; and religion and philosophy. The collection also includes thousands of important works from the Americas.

The eighteenth century has been called "The Age of Enlightenment." It was a period of rapid advance in print culture and publishing, in world exploration, and in the rapid growth of science and technology – all of which had a profound impact on the political and cultural landscape. At the end of the century the American Revolution, French Revolution and Industrial Revolution, perhaps three of the most significant events in modern history, set in motion developments that eventually dominated world political, economic, and social life.

In a groundbreaking effort, Gale initiated a revolution of its own: digitization of epic proportions to preserve these invaluable works in the largest online archive of its kind. Contributions from major world libraries constitute over 175,000 original printed works. Scanned images of the actual pages, rather than transcriptions, recreate the works *as they first appeared.*

Now for the first time, these high-quality digital scans of original works are available via print-on-demand, making them readily accessible to libraries, students, independent scholars, and readers of all ages.

For our initial release we have created seven robust collections to form one the world's most comprehensive catalogs of 18th century works.

Initial Gale ECCO Print Editions collections include:

History and Geography
Rich in titles on English life and social history, this collection spans the world as it was known to eighteenth-century historians and explorers. Titles include a wealth of travel accounts and diaries, histories of nations from throughout the world, and maps and charts of a world that was still being discovered. Students of the War of American Independence will find fascinating accounts from the British side of conflict.

Social Science

Delve into what it was like to live during the eighteenth century by reading the first-hand accounts of everyday people, including city dwellers and farmers, businessmen and bankers, artisans and merchants, artists and their patrons, politicians and their constituents. Original texts make the American, French, and Industrial revolutions vividly contemporary.

Medicine, Science and Technology

Medical theory and practice of the 1700s developed rapidly, as is evidenced by the extensive collection, which includes descriptions of diseases, their conditions, and treatments. Books on science and technology, agriculture, military technology, natural philosophy, even cookbooks, are all contained here.

Literature and Language

Western literary study flows out of eighteenth-century works by Alexander Pope, Daniel Defoe, Henry Fielding, Frances Burney, Denis Diderot, Johann Gottfried Herder, Johann Wolfgang von Goethe, and others. Experience the birth of the modern novel, or compare the development of language using dictionaries and grammar discourses.

Religion and Philosophy

The Age of Enlightenment profoundly enriched religious and philosophical understanding and continues to influence present-day thinking. Works collected here include masterpieces by David Hume, Immanuel Kant, and Jean-Jacques Rousseau, as well as religious sermons and moral debates on the issues of the day, such as the slave trade. The Age of Reason saw conflict between Protestantism and Catholicism transformed into one between faith and logic -- a debate that continues in the twenty-first century.

Law and Reference

This collection reveals the history of English common law and Empire law in a vastly changing world of British expansion. Dominating the legal field is the *Commentaries of the Law of England* by Sir William Blackstone, which first appeared in 1765. Reference works such as almanacs and catalogues continue to educate us by revealing the day-to-day workings of society.

Fine Arts

The eighteenth-century fascination with Greek and Roman antiquity followed the systematic excavation of the ruins at Pompeii and Herculaneum in southern Italy; and after 1750 a neoclassical style dominated all artistic fields. The titles here trace developments in mostly English-language works on painting, sculpture, architecture, music, theater, and other disciplines. Instructional works on musical instruments, catalogs of art objects, comic operas, and more are also included.

The BiblioLife Network

This project was made possible in part by the BiblioLife Network (BLN), a project aimed at addressing some of the huge challenges facing book preservationists around the world. The BLN includes libraries, library networks, archives, subject matter experts, online communities and library service providers. We believe every book ever published should be available as a high-quality print reproduction; printed on-demand anywhere in the world. This insures the ongoing accessibility of the content and helps generate sustainable revenue for the libraries and organizations that work to preserve these important materials.

The following book is in the "public domain" and represents an authentic reproduction of the text as printed by the original publisher. While we have attempted to accurately maintain the integrity of the original work, there are sometimes problems with the original work or the micro-film from which the books were digitized. This can result in minor errors in reproduction. Possible imperfections include missing and blurred pages, poor pictures, markings and other reproduction issues beyond our control. Because this work is culturally important, we have made it available as part of our commitment to protecting, preserving, and promoting the world's literature.

GUIDE TO FOLD-OUTS MAPS and OVERSIZED IMAGES

The book you are reading was digitized from microfilm captured over the past thirty to forty years. Years after the creation of the original microfilm, the book was converted to digital files and made available in an online database.

In an online database, page images do not need to conform to the size restrictions found in a printed book. When converting these images back into a printed bound book, the page sizes are standardized in ways that maintain the detail of the original. For large images, such as fold-out maps, the original page image is split into two or more pages

Guidelines used to determine how to split the page image follows:

• Some images are split vertically; large images require vertical and horizontal splits.
• For horizontal splits, the content is split left to right.
• For vertical splits, the content is split from top to bottom.
• For both vertical and horizontal splits, the image is processed from top left to bottom right.

8494 dc.24

INSTRUCTIONS

To a

SON,

Containing

RULES of CONDUCT in publick
and private LIFE,

Under the following Heads.

Religion Marriage The Court Friendship Travelling Housekeeping and Hospitality. Tenants and	other Concerns of Estate Study and Exercise Of Pleasure, Idleness, &c.

By ARCHIBALD Marquis of *ARGYLE.*

Address'd to his Children, and to his eldest Son in
particular.

Written in the Year 1660, during his Confinement.

To which are added by the same Noble AUTHOR:

General Maxims of Life Maxims Political and Military, under the following heads. The Prince War.	Courage Command. Fortune Victory Miscellaneous Observations.

GLASGOW:

Printed by R FOULIS, and sold by him there, at *Edinburgh,* by Mess HAMILTON and BALFOUR 1743

THE

MARQUIS of

ARGYLE's

INSTRUCTIONS

To his SON.

SON,

I Know there are feveral books in print, written prudently, politick-ly, and pioufly, of this very title, of late years. I confefs, moft of them were of particular intendment to their own relations, the reafon probably that they are not of fuch general ob-fervation and ufe; others defigned out of prefumptuous ambition, of exceeding by imitation fuch rare pat-terns as went before, in the accef-

A   fions

fions of wit and elegant difcourfe,
difcoloured fometimes with urbane,
facete prophanenefs.

I do acknowledge 'tis a fingular
and the right way of tranfmitting of
a man's memory to pofterity, efpecially to his own; it argues a kind of reverence that men bear to themfelves,
when they can fo impartially unbo-
fom themfelves in the account and
register of all their actions, and can
fhew no difliked experience of them,
as to their own proper guilt. I do
not hereby underftand what concerns religion; who can excufe or
extenuate his failings? but of moral
tranfient acts, to the evil of which
no man is fo ftrongly inclinable, but
by the biafs of a corrupt education.

Many very fententious pieces are
extant among ancient authors of this
fubject, but I know none teftamen-
tary but among the moderns, and of
them we have fome excellent princes, and renowned ftatefmen.

My care of you, whom I would
have to confider yourfelf, as the
prop

prop of an ancient honourable Family, is no way leſs than theirs, however I am inferior to them in dignity and judgment: and therefore I will trace a beaten way, rather than loſe myſelf and you in a general diſcourſe; what I come ſhort of here, you cannot miſs in their common places, and ſo I may be ſure I ſhall attain my end.

Probably men may think I can add nothing to that ſtore, but if they conſider my ſtation, and how far concerned in theſe times, they may rather expect novel politicks from me, ſuch a variation of the latitude of the moſt approved and received maxims of ſtate lying in the ſphere in which I acted; but the managery of the counſels of thoſe times, were by ſucceſs, or the monſtrous guilt and fraud of the politicians, ſo irregular, that I cannot if I would, bring them under heads, though up and down as they occur I may point at them.

I confeſs, it was my great misfor-

A 2   tune

tune to be so deeply engaged in these
fatal times; I know the nobility of
Scotland have always bickered with
their princes, and from the insolency
of that custom, not any of our kings
have been free. 'Tis also true, the
perpetual family-feuds among us,
which by all the industry and authority of our princes, could never be
so pacified, but that they revived a-
gain, and took upon themselves, as
they had advantage, to revenge their
quarrel; (and yet like sudden floods
which violently over-run, and as
peaceably return within their banks,
abated to their due allegiance,) did
easily persuade me that there was no
such apparent danger in the first beginnings of the contest, betwixt the
king and my nation of *Scotland.* I
had laid it for a maxim, that a reformation was sooner effected *per gla-*
dium oris, than *per os gladii;* and certainly true religion is rather a settler,
than stickler in policy, and rather
confirms men in obedience to the
government established, than invites
them

them to the erecting of new; which
they neither do nor can know,
till it be discovered and declared.
Wherein I did not look upon our
intended reformation as any way
taxable, since it had the whole stream
of universal consent of the whole
nation; I never thought of those
dire consequences which presently
followed, till by that confusion my
thoughts became distracted, and my-
self encountred so many difficulties
in the way, that all remedies that
were applied had the quite contrary
operation, whatever therefore hath
been said by me and others in this
matter, you must repute and accept
them as from a distracted man, of a
distracted subject, in a distracted
time wherein I lived: And this shall
serve to let you know how far I
waded unwarily in that business.

I will not however counsel you,
if any such lamentable commotions
(which God forbid) should break
out, for my unhappiness, to with-
draw yourself, from interposing to
quench

quench and allay them as much as
by your authority you can, (however I was miftaken by fome in my
actions, I did labour for a right underftanding,) but be fure let your allegiance keep the ballance; by no
means ftand like a neuter in the
caufe of your king and country.
That decree of *Solon*'s, That every
man that in a general commotion
was of neither party, fhould be ad-
judged infamous, is rightly decreed
of great men. Popular furies would
never have end, if not awed by their
fuperiors, who fupinely neglecting
fuch outrages, not feldom, are
ruined and deprefs'd in their own e-
ftates and honours; a late example
whereof we had in our neighbour
nation; the people will foon learn
their own ftrength, that *fumma po-
teftas radicatur in voluntatibus hominum;* and from thence infer, that
the popular power excells the power
of the noblelfe.

Great men therefore, are in fome
fort as neceffary as good men, as
power

power is as requisite as wisdom; where they are both wanting, *imperium in imperio quaerendum est.* Your famous ancestors by both these, have kept their vassals (and what is well done in one canton of the kingdom is like to be imitated throughout,) in a quiet subjection, and good comportment many generations, and I question not but you will find the same reverence from them, if you do not degenerate.

Do not content yourself with the bare titles of greatness, *principis tantum nomen habere non est esse princeps;* that power is vain which never exerts itself forth into act.

The looseness of these late times will require at first a gentle hand, when you have got the bridle in the mouths of your family, dependents and vassals, then you may curb them, and reduce them to the former obedience they once willingly paid. I have had a difficult task with them, yet by one means or other I kept

them

them in order ; nor will they be ever serviceable to their supreme, if they be not in a due subjection to you, their immediate lord.

Take all fair occasions of doing your sovereign service, let that be your only emulation with other noble houses, supply the great and necessary distance of your prince from this his native kingdom, by a close application of yourself to his concerns, if not in a publick capacity, yet in your private sphere, which will soon advance you to higher trusts.

You have a great task to do, you must from the bottom climb up to the mount of honour, a very abrupt and difficult ascent; which yet, nevertheless, by observing the sure footings of some of your progenitors, and the slips of others, particularly those recent slidings of mine own, (for other they are not) you may at last attain the top, and by your own merit and your prince's favour, your house may be culminant again.

If

If it shall so happen, as I despair not of it, ancient merit with good princes (such as without flattery I may say the most of ours were and are like to be,) will out-last their longest displeasure, have a care then of that precipice, let no revenge or ambition blind you into destruction; you may poise yourself with your wings of honour and greatness, but venture not, nor presume to fly.

Covet not with immoderate haste lands, riches, honour, for it is seldom that men, whose rash desires and designs are laid out that way, compass their full content, and for the most part meet with a destiny far other than they expected; and when they are once so disappointed, fortune or rather Providence so much amazeth the judgment even of wise men, as in time of danger they know not what resolution is best to be taken. You will not be necessitated through the want of these three, so as to reach at them unlawfully, and

B　　　　endan-

endanger what you have in poffeffion, and yourfelf together.

I do not much regret your private
life, nor fhould I labour to bring you
into ftate-employment, for there is
no courfe more comely, nor any re-
folution fo well befeeming a wife
man, having made proof of his own
virtue, as to retire himfelf from
court and company, for fo he fhall
fhun the inconveniencies of contempt,
and the difcommodity of a perpetual
trouble.

I have tried and found the many
perplexities that attend that life, and
have reaped nothing but calumny
and envy, though I do not fay this
is the fate of all ftatifts; this I am
fure, the beft way of coming there,
is without popular fame or over-
vogued merit, efpecially by the intereft of a favourite.

But whofo cannot endure the envy and hate that are the attendants
thereof, muft fit down with his prefent condition, and not meddle with,
or enterprife great matters, for great

ho-

honours being defired of many, it is
of neceffity that he that afpireth unto them, muft be for his advancement thereunto envied, and for his
authority hated, which, although
they be well managed and ufed, yet
thofe who hate and envy, perfuading
themfelves they might be better hand-
led, endeavour to opprefs that power
as fearing it might be worfe.

You will have time after the fet-
tling of your own private fortunes
to caft about for fome honourable
advantages for yourfelf. Time is
the beft counfellor, rather let magi-
ftracy want you, than you want it;
which you may effect, if by a wife
moderation you can flight thofe *in-
fignia* which the world knows your
anceftors have born with commen-
dation and honour, and who have
added more luftre to them, than the
want of them can take from you.

Keep a firm and amicable corre-
fpondence with your neighbours
howfoever, but fo that it be far from
giving any fufpicion of making par-

ties

ties or factions, this is chiefly attained by a generous compliance and noble familiarity, that's the way to be loved and honoured, which works so many good effects, as daily experience sufficeth without any express example to prove them of great force. If you be happy in this particular, this will be your certain repose, and may not be reckoned within the *externa bona fortunae.*

To compass this, take an exact care that your actions be just, be not offended at every injury, wink sometimes at your wrong, but beware of unnecessary revenges. I leave you enemies enough, 'twill be meat and drink (as the English proverb) to them, to see you froward and quarrelsom; bear off all the affronts that be put upon you with an inviolable invincible mind, and let them see you are above them. Master all your passions and affections, and so discipline them that they may become your most necessary servants.

You will be freed, by this your
retire-

retirement from publick employment, of adulation and flattery, and by that means will the better and more plainly and sincerely converse with yourself, and be able to give a near judgment what you are, and of your abilities and defects, which is the most necessary knowledge in the world, and which will recompense the disuse of other policy, *è coelo descendit,* γνῶθι σεαυτὸν.

Demean yourself in an equality of mind, that may show fortune hath no power over you, that her excesses and recesses, her over-flows nor her low ebbs, can either drown or dry up your virtue. 'Tis but common fate; as the sea loseth in one place it gets in another; so contrarily, such shakings as these which through me befal my family, may by your prudence rivet it faster.

This I thought fit in general, as to the condition I shall leave you in, to direct and advise you; only one word more. I charge you to forget,
and

and not harbour any animofity or particular anger againft any man concerning me. Such heart-burnings have been the deftruction of many a noble perfon in this kingdom, and I know not of any perfon fo given, but the very fame meafure hath been meted unto him again. The Cup is gone round, and therefore content yourfelf; but above all I require you to have more regard to Chriftianity, than covertly or bafely to kill a particular enemy by fecret affault or practice, it being altogether moft unwarrantable either by faith or honour.

And this by way of premife.

To

To the reft of his CHILDREN.

Children,

AS you are the gieateft pait of me, and in whom I may pio-mife to myfelf a continuance of fuc-ceffion, fo have I alfo a paternal care (more incumbent on me now) to-wards you. I fhall therefore in fome particular directions to you, as the monuments of my affection, advife and counfel you, in what fhall be neceffary and expedient for your fe-veral conditions.

Firft, Theiefoie, make not hafte to put yourfelves out of the govern-ment or charge of thofe to whofe care and tuition I have committed you; if any thing happen that fhall offer you advantage in another fta-tion of life, than I leave you, I re-quire you to confult with them firft. I have laid a facred obligation upon them to affift and aid you in all mat-ters, which if you neglect or con-

temn,

temn, you will foon find yourfelves
left to the world, as a fhip to the
raging fea, without furniture or an-
chors.

Above all, bear that conftant filial
duty to your mother, which her piety and tendernefs in your education, moft juftly call for at your
hands; her great indulgence towards
you, and her entire affection to me
in all my fuffering of late, deferve
very much at my hand; and therefore I charge you to fhew that re-
fpect to her for me, which I would
have done myfelf, and in which,
in all the time of our wedlock you
have known me to have continued.
Fail not in any outward circum-
ftance of honour and reverence to
her, that fo by your dutiful behaviour and carriage towards her, fome
of the harfhnefs and afperity of her
prefent condition may be alleviated.

To your eldeft brother, who is
the prince of your family, fhew
yourfelves obedient and loving; he
is my fubftitute, your honour is
bound

bound up in his, in him it now
rests, and may for a while not ap-
pear in its lustre, take heed therefore you do not by any disrespect
quite extinguish it, your due observance of him will preserve it in the
minds of all men, who are not strangers to the ancient worth and merit
of *our House.*

With one another maintain a mutual love and confidence. This happiness you may have by my adversity to indear yourselves more to one
another, lay out no affection upon
the world, but keep the entire stock
for yourselves. Let that equal love
which I bear you, and which I leave
with you, be communicated among
you, by a constant amity to one another; which will be the better ce-
mented by your religious and godly
conversation, wherein I trust you
have been so well instructed, that
my memory shall not be charged
or blamed for your education.

Keep a decorum in your present
condition, value not yourselves the

worse

worfe for one riot or attempt of fortune made upon me, mind not her
temporary outrages ; virtue is the
true ftandard, fuch allays pafs not
with her, fix yourfelves upon your
own worth, and no engine of fate
can remove you from that bafis.
Pufillanimity is a vice almoft needlefs to be warned of, becaufe noble
minds do always *niti contra*, and
bear up againft their extremities,
till they have either furmounted them
by their bravery, and afcended to
their firft height; or levelled them
by their patience and equanimity,
plain'd their difficulties, and made
them even with their contented
minds.

The fmall portions I have left
you, (though the world mifcounts
them as great matters, and I could
wifh they amounted to their fums)
you muft improve as talents ; ferve
your neceffities with them, not your
pleafures ; what the royal bounty
may hereafter do by way of reftitution, you may do with it as may be
moft

moft fubfervient to your honour; you will not be liable to great expences, you are free from any dependency on court, where men fpend money, on a vanity called hope. As for marriage, (of which I fhall fpeak more largely hereafter, and of which in the beginning of this monition, I gave you a caution,) your virtue muft fupply dower; though I truft I have left a competency (with your virtues) to match you to any family in *Scotland.*

Behave yourfelves therefore prudently, decently, and warily to all people, that fo you may gain the general good-will and benevolence of all; imitate the example your mother hath fet before you, ftand upon your guard againft all pleafures, or other baits or allurements, that fhall tempt you to any unlawful actions or defires, which may practife upon you either in your confcience, or in your reputation. and refolve this as a fure rule with

C 2 your-

yourfelves, that no perfon is wife or safe, but he that is honeft.

Fear your Creator, and ferve him with all your might; begin all your works and actions with him, 'tis he only can fucceed and profper them. If you purfue your own defigns upon your own bottom, the conclufion will be your own ruin, for he can wither and blaft at his pleafure finful undertakings. I fhall never defpair of God's blefling upon you, nor doubt his All-fufficiency for you, if you apply yourfelves to him, and make his fear the rule of your lives.

You fee that to be defcended of great perfonages, is no exemption from the ftrokes of fortune; but to be defcended of a heavenly race, will carry you out of the reach of thofe misfortunes which are incident to humanity.

Imploy therefore your time in renewing your alliances there; probably your confanguinity and relations here, may ftand off from you,

like

like *Job*'s friends in his adversity. Desertions are usual in this case; you need however not much care for this worldly friendship, as long as you have dependence on the favour of Heaven.

What is abated here to you in the transitory felicities and pleasures of the world, (from which you have no such cause to wean yourselves altogether) will be easily recompensed in your enjoying him who is the foundation of all good, and from whom all happiness is derived to his creatures.

To whose protection I commit you and your ways, beseeching him to bless and prosper them, to his glory, and your comfort.

CHAP.

CHAP. I.

RELIGION.

THIS being your greateſt con-
cernment, the director of all
your actions, I cannot uſe my paternal authority to better purpoſe, than
in adjuring you and ſtraightly charg-
ing and requiring you, to be conſtant
and zealous in the religion now left
eſtabliſhed in this kingdom. I will
not take upon me now to decide
controverſies ariſen betwixt ours and
the church of *England* in matters of
diſcipline, they agreeing altogether
in doctrine; all that I ſhall ſay is,
that their ceremonies have not been
uſed here, and you have been bred
up without them, and the nation of
Scotland otherwiſe affected, and
therefore, you ſhall do well to continue in this kirk; though I would
rather have it your own choice, than
any

any other confideration whatfoever. Diverfity in any thing diftracteth the mind, and leaves it waving in a dubious perplexity, and then how eafy is it to fway the mind to either fide? this is moft true and experienced in religion, you muft therefore obfirmate your ears, and confirm your judgment, being once fatisfied of the excellency of your profeffion, and having received the true and fincere doctrine.

Neither would I have you only fixt and conftant in your religion, but alfo very devout in the practice of it; that as heretofore your anceftors have been eminent for honour, you that come fhort of them by this *deliquium* or eclipfe of it in me, may neverthelefs exceed them in the true way to it, by your zeal and piety: and remember this, that he that is not truly religious, will hardly be efteemed fuch, fince nothing is of lefs continuance than hypocrify and diffimulation; and if your religion be fuch, fuch will your greatnefs and

honour

honour be, a feigned thing and a mere shadow.

The observance of religion, and the exercise of good manners, do become none so much as illustrious persons; other glories have lifted them beyond the pitch and reach of men, but this is a ray of the Divinity which advanceth them near to the Deity; and like the diamond out-shines the lustre of all other jewels. A religious heart and a clear conscience will make you truly conspicuous; it is as the mother of all other virtues; what brave effects of obedience to princes hath it wrought in subjects? look back to the primitive times and the emperors, how courageous were they in all enterprizes, hardy and resolute in dangers, liberal to their necessities, ready to do their utmost devoir in the distress affairs of the empire? and this from one pious principle, that in serving their prince, they served God, whose lieutenant he is, nor was

was there any difficulty over which their faith did not triumph.

Neverthelefs, fome have taxed, and it hath been a long and ftrong imputation, that this kirk of *Scotland*, doth teach fedition againft, or at leaft the diminution of the authority of their princes. For my part I know no fuch matter, nor did I ever embrace or adhere to fuch opinions, though cenfured for them, if any man's Intemperature hath vented fuch dangerous tenets, or his rafh prefumption ventilated fuch queftions, I have nothing to do with them, I difown and difclaim them; and therefore to remove this prejudice from you alfo, I charge you to make your duty to your fovereign one of the chief points of your religion, fo far forth as it may confift with your obedience to God, who ought to be ferved beft, and in the firft place. There is fuch a reciprocation between both thofe fervices, that commonly they go together.

D What-

Whatever the late miſcarriages have been by the people's ſtruggling for their liberty of conſcience, as they are paſt, ſo they have left the means whereby they may be prevented for the future: and no doubt the good temperament of the king, with an eaſy indulgent hand of his miniſters, will keep religion from the ſcandal of a civil war.

'Tis a maxim of ſtate, that where princes and people are of a different religion, they will not well agree; yet modern experience, and ſince the reformation arrived to a ſettled conſtitution and church-government, evinceth the contrary; as at preſent in the kingdom of *France*, and in *Germany*, where the quite oppoſite religions are peaceably and quietly profeſt. But God be thanked, there is no ſuch contrariety in the religion profeſſed in theſe two neighbouring kingdoms, which may not (without animoſity and intereſt keep the breach open,) be reconciled; all impatient

patient zeal being turned into an e-mulation of loyalty to the king.

Cherish and maintain the mini-sters of the gospel, especially, pain-ful able preachers. Nothing brings more contempt upon, or aviles reli-gion, and the service of God, in the eyes of the vulgar, than the necessi-ties, wants and miseries of church-men, what esteem you confer upon them, will soon redound and reflect again upon you. What the heathen said of their poets, that by their means and writings, famous men were transmitted to immortality, who otherwise would have lain in perpetual oblivion, is very true of evangelical doctors, their prayers, and their instructions, and their re-commendations of you, together with your own endeavour after holiness, which is the only fame and glory, will transmit and place you hereafter in heaven, and establish you here, living and dead, in the good-will and praise of all men.

Let charity be a chief ingredient

in

in your religion, both in giving and forgiving. As you shall have abilities, indulge the poor, and let them in some measure partake with you in your outward blessings and enjoyments. For the other, as you are always liable to offences, so be always as apt and prone to pardon or pass them by, which in the greatest adversities you can undergo, will never be out of your power to do.

Frequent the church and the houses of God; let no business invade or intrude upon your religious hours; what you have destined to the service of God, is already sacred to him, and cannot without great profaneness be alienated from him, and conferred upon others; use private prayers, as well as go to the publick ordinances.

For other duties necessary for a Christian's practice, I refer you to the discipline and instructions of the kirk; it being needless to repeat them here, being so exactly laid down

by

by her, whom I take to be the pureſt church.

For ſearch all religions through the world, and you will find none that aſcribes ſo much to God, nor that conſtitutes ſuch a firm love among men, as does the eſtabliſh'd doctrine, (I except the ſchiſms amongſt us) of the Proteſtant church among you: In whoſe arms I leave you, and her to the everlaſting protection and guidance of God.

CHAP.

C H A P. II.

Of Marriage.

HAving devoted yourself prin-
cipally to the service of God,
and subordinately to your prince,
which includes your country; the
next duty or affection, you owe to
yourself in the ordering or governing of your life, according to your
several inclinations and dispositions.
And among the most important and
strong sways of nature, I reckon
marriage, especially in great and
noble families, where interest for-
bids perpetual virginity; nor ever
since the suppressing of nunneries,
and such monastick privacies and re-
nunciations to the world, have we
had in this kingdom, many, if any
of the daughters of *Jephtha.*

Marriage no doubt was one of
the greatest favours that God conferred

ferred on mankind, and when he
beſtows a virtuous mate, whoſe hu-
mility, chaſtity and affection, are e-
minently great, he doth renew his
firſt intentions of kindneſs to man,
and gives grace upon grace, and infinitely happy is he that can find
and make ſuch a choice. 'Twas
therefore well ſaid by him, that diſ-
courſing of this ſubject, affirmed that
God did oftentimes reward the good
works, the honeſty and piety of a
man, by the offer and tender of a
good wife, for parents could only
give wealth and riches, lands and
eſtates to their children, but God
only could give them prudent and
diſcreet women.

In the contracting therefore of
marriage, virtue is more to be con-
ſidered than money; beauty will ri-
val with either of them, and oftentimes gets poſſeſſion ſooner than
both; but then it quickly loſeth it
again, as having not thoſe ſtays and
ſupportations which each of the o-
ther have in themſelves.

I

I acknowledge, virtue is firft to be courted, and the *primitiae*, the firft fruits of our love fhould be offered up at her fhrines; but yet referving the ftock to facrifice to the numerous contingencies and accidents, which befall the wedded ftate, by the additional helps of handfomenefs and wealth.

But be not overblinded with beauty, 'tis one of the greateft deceits nature is guilty of; not that it is fo in thofe perfons to whom fhe is gracioufly and liberally pleafed to beftow it, (for 'tis the moft exact copy of her illuftrious felf,) but in the fafcination and witchery it darts through the eyes into the minds of men; you cannot but pay homage to it, but let that tribute redeem you from a total conqueft. Remember, that it is but clay, more refined and fet off with a better varnifh, and being all on the outfide, lies open to weather and confuming time, and fometimes to prefent misfortunes; while that which is internal

nal

nal stands the shock, and endures
all brunts, like a strong fortified
garrison, when the other shews like
a weak gay army in the field, ready
to be vanquished at the first encounter.

Money is the sinew of love, as
well as war, you can do nothing
happily in wedlock without it, the
other are court-cards, but they are
not of the trump-suit, and are foiled
by every sneaking misadventure, virtue is suppreft, and cannot emerge
and dilate itself in the streights of a
narrow fortune, and beauty is be-
trayed to the necessity of keeping it
fo; otherwise in a pinching condition, leanness and dead paleness
would usurp the place where full-
blown roses sat with love before.
Nor was it ever known, that a beau-
tiful woman driven to want, escaped
the offers and importunities of men,
who under the pretence of pitying
and supplying her distresses, by de-
grees have gain'd upon her honour
and pudicity, while she satisfies her-

E   felf,

felf, that out of (miferable) gratitude fhe could do no lefs.

I do much approve of crofs-marriages between families, which have been fo allied for many defcents together, fo as they be not in that proximity in which the houfe of *Auftria* matches. By the race we guefs of the production,—— *De fortibus creantur fortes,*—— and that adds a firm monument to both houfes, being fo incorporated into one another. However men reckon it for glory in heraldry, to bear almoft the whole arms of the kingdom in one efcutcheon; methinks honour there looks like a river, which branched into feveral rivulets lofeth itfelf in them; whereas ftreams that take in another large confluent, carry all before them, and run directly into the ocean, and difembogue themfelves with a name.

If you are not affected that way, there is variety enough in *Scotland*; but whatever you do, confult with your honour firft, do not embafe

your

your blood by matching below you, it will foon breed diftafte and diflike in yourfelf, which will caufe malice and revenge in her, and entail contempt upon your iffue and pofterity. Such embraces will be like the twining of the ivy about the oak, fuck up moifture from the root, while the branches are withered, and the ftock falls to the ground, never like to reflourifh again.

As you match your Peer in honour, let her be fo in years; a difference in age is a fecret fire raked up for a time, which will afterwards break out and confume your quiet: when either of your defires and ftrength anfwer not the vigour of the youngeft, then the fparkles will fly by fuch violent collifions and clafhings that will foon fet your family in combuftion.

After your choice made and pitch'd upon, and a vow paffed, keep yourfelf religioufly to it, (the breach whereof, is a vulgar common fin in *Scotland*, and therefore the more detestable

teftable

teſtable to you) knowing there can
be no diſpenſation from it, and nothing but miſery after it joyned with
ſhame and repentance.

In the ſtate of marriage carry
yourſelf affectionately and diſcreet-
ly; and keep ſtrictly the rites of it,
that no jealouſy, that canker-worm
of conjugal love, fret that ſilken
knot which tied you together. Owe
nothing to one another in zeal and
fervency of affection, which will
ſoon beget ſuch a mutual confidence, that the reſt of your life will
be but an advantageous repetition of
your firſt joys, and add number to
your contents and pleaſures, as to
your years.

Let not the ſecrets of marriage
paſs beyond the chamber; for he
little regards his own honour or his
wife's chaſtity, who blazes or diſ-
covers what is done there; and no
ſlyer debauchery is there to women,
than what by ſuch luxuriant freedom of their husbands tongues, is
                              prompted

prompted to their wandring and strong imaginations.

I pray for, and wish your good success in this great affair, and commend you to him, who is only able to grant it you.

C H A P.

C H A P. III.

Of the Court.

YOU are not thither bound, and I am not forry you are forbidden refort thither, as to any employment or traffick: 'tis a place difficult of accefs, fhut up with rocks, fhallows, and fands, and not one adventurer in twenty comes off a faver. Befides, 'tis a place of a moft uncertain air, full of damps and exhalations, fpread with clouds and over-caft, and fometimes again fcorching hot, in the fudden rife and depreffion of favourites.

But if your curiofity fhall invite you to the danger, when time may look with a better afpect upon you, remember thefe obfervations of mine own, who both at diftance, and at clofe view have well confidered it.

Firft then, as to the favour of
your

your prince, which is the moft de-
firable thing in the world, 'tis rather
an illuftrious care, than a content-
ful poffeffion, nor do wife men ever
bufy themfelves about it, becaufe
the tranquillity of fpirit, which they
feek for, is not to be found amidft
the confufions of the court. and to
guard a man's felf from the misfortunes there, and the envy which the
graces of princes do contract upon
their favourites, there is no way better than privacy and retirednefs. You
muft know that 'tis mere human
weaknefs, which caufeth princes to
raife favourites, to aid and fupport
them in the weight and multitude of
affairs, and fometimes in fuch fecrets
which are heavier upon the mind
than all the reft; the fad effect
whereof every age hath given an example.

You muft at your entrance, refolve to encounter the accofts of contempt, fcorn, difcontents and repul-
fes, with a bold fore-head, and take
no notice of flightings and injuries
done

done you by the great ones. A
thing I alwys judged grievous to a
generous mind; and yet thefe are ordinarily the fteps to preferment.

If you fhall find favour at court,
beware your covetoufnefs after new
boons, make you not forget the old
ones; and if then you receive deni-
als, guard yourfelf, that the diftafte
be not more prevalent to run you
into actions of dangerous confe-
quence, than reafon can be to keep
you in your duty.

Extraordinary diligence and affected affiduity are to no purpofe,
whereby men think *to prevene their
advancement; on the contrary, if
men neglect and feem carelefs of pro-
motion, attending when the merit of
their actions fhall offer it them, time
or fortune feldom fail to conduct
them to true and permanent glory.

It hath been an old adage, *A
young courtier, an old beggar;* men
fpending eftates in riot in fuch confuming places as cities, in a fruitlefs
                                    ex-

---

* To forward.

expectation, and then carry home nothing but repentance.

A cholerick person is not fit to be a courtier, for if he should go about to revenge himself of the indignities, bravado's, deceits, and tricks put upon him, he shall suffer more in an hour, than he shall be satisfied for in ten years.

You must do at *Rome*, what others do there, be sure to sing no other airs than which most please the prince. 'Twas *Solon's* comparison of courtiers, who resembled them to counters, with which men use to cast accounts, for, as in changing their places, they stand sometimes for more, sometimes for less; so princes do the same with them, now advancing them in honour and dignity, and presently debasing them at their pleasure to the scorn and derision of all men, so that it is truly said, that men have an opportunity of losing themselves at court, and of finding themselves at home.

Old courtiers are like old ships,

F brought

brought into harbours and there laid up, never to be put to sea to any new adventure.

'Tis a tart sarcasm or satyrical pass upon the court, that one said; At the court are bishops and priests to baptize, and change names; for there, the vain-glorious ambitious man, is called honourable; the prodigal, magnificent; the coward, wise; the wise, hypocrite; the malicious, subtile; the adulterous, amorous; the covetous, temperate; and what confidence can any man repose in friends there, whose greatness renders them the more intractable? 'Tis very difficult to find virtue at court; but it is more difficult to keep it.

He that sins and repents, and returns again to his sin, sins more grossly than at first; so to leave the court, and return again, is such an error that is not excuseable, save with this, that the return was to sell virtue, and gain wealth; since it is a great kindness of fortune or puissance of virtue, to escape that gulf.

Against

Againft the envy of the court as againft the plague, there is no better prefervative, than reticat and eloingment; a remedy practifed very often but with different fuccefs; it being very dangerous for popular perfons, and fuch as have had great commands, to abfent themfelves without leave or difmiffion; for it not only breeds fufpicions and jealoufies of their difaffection, and confequently of the danger of a rebellion; but likewife expofeth them to the unobftructed defigns and malice of their enemies, which feldom end but in ruin.

This is generally the complaint of courts; wherein you muft underftand there is not the leaft concurrence of the prince to give any fuch caufe for it, but that by tradition the grandees walk by it as by a rule; and fince monarchy was, court-arts have been, and can vie precedency with any myftery. I never knew any great favourite, who practifed any new ways of his own: fome have been nobler and more

magni-

magnificent than others, freer in access and more affable, but yet still kept close to their court-lessons, nor could ever their private virtues gain upon their publick concerns.

It is possible a man may get an estate at court, but it is more probable he may lose one, that which is got there, through how many curses and imprecations it passeth, that which is lost, with how many woes, and tears, and deprecations goes it ' so much is a court worse than a lottery.

While you can therefore pay your devotion, your loyalty to your prince at home, and probably be better accepted; what need have you of a dangerous unnecessary pilgrimage to the shrine, to pay a personal adoration' your oblation there can be nothing less than your quiet and estate, in lieu whereof they will present you with a trinket or some other bauble, which you will be ashamed to carry home again.

Fear God, honour the king, live at home, and love your neighbours.

CHAP.

CHAP. IV.

Of Friendſhip.

S o n,

AS you have not that ranging freedom of choice of your ſociety; ſuſpicion on the one hand, and reaſon of ſtate on the other hedging you up, and impaling you within a narrow ſcantling ; ſo neither can the iniquity of any the worſt fortune leave a man in ſuch a ſolitude, in which a guide, a friend, (by whoſe counſels and ſweet converſe, either he may extricate himſelf from, or avoid the tediouſneſs of his troubles,) may not be had. What therefore you ſhall lack in the multitude of friends, who like flies faſten on the ſweets of honour, fame, riches, &c. you will find no great loſs in, if it be your happineſs to
find

find out but one or two, (such an oligarchy of friendship,) whose unity in affection and fidelity, will richly compensate the many cyphers that attend on greatness.

To make a right choice therefore, you must first propose to yourself the inconstancy of man, the most changeable, alterable creature in the world. Every breath of wind fans him to a various shape; think not therefore of making a friendship fixt and eternal. How ardently have men loved some, even beyond the desire of dying for them, when in a moment, as it were one hasty ebullition of choler hath render'd them exceeding offensive, nay, hath sunk them into our hate and execration? see the fast hold which man doth take of man! 'tis let go and unfastned in a moment, by the clacking of the tongue, a nod, a frown, or such like nothing; we cancel leagues with friends, make new ones with enemies, and break them ere concluded. The consideration of this will keep

you

you from overweening any man,
and from a total truft and confidence
in him, and beget in you a feverer
exercife of, and confequently a firmer reliance on your own virtues and
abilities.

Nothing fooner corrupts or rottens
friendfhip, than an over-hafty enter-
taining of it, like præcoce fruit that's
ripe before its feafon. Judgment is
the only cement that clofeth and
binds the affections of men. where
that's wanting, 'tis like building with
untempered mortar, the ftructure's
like to fall on our own head. I never knew any yet fo good, but fome
have thought him vile, and hated
him; nor contrarily, any fo bad but
fome have thought him honeft, and
loved him; either the ignorance, the
envy, or the partiality of thofe that
judge, do conftitute a various man:
in fome, report hath fore-blinded
judgment; in fome, accident is the
caufe of difpofing us to love or hate.
The foul is often led by fecret un-
inveftigable ways and motions to
love,

love, fhe knows not why. But 'tis time alone and long probation, which feldom fail to give right information, when nature, art and report may deceive you. Every man may keep his mind, if he lifts, in a labyrinth. 'Tis a room by us infcrutable, into which nature has made no certain window, but as he himfelf fhall pleafe to give you light, which is in fuch tranfient glimmerings that it rarely ftrikes any thing but the eye, leaving us immediately to grope again in the dark.

I remit you to your own experience; you have converfed in the world (troublefome enough for many years) with all forts and all humours of perfons; but for your better guidance herein, I fhall give you thefe properties of friendfhip, which my longer obfervation hath found to be true characters of it.

He who is really your friend, will give you counfel before you afk it; and that's the reafon a man cannot

not

not keep a friend by constraint, nor oblige secrecy by coercion.

Most men regard their profit, and therefore use their friends as men use beasts, carefully attend and look to them, from whom they receive increase and advantages, and so deny themselves, and want the most desirable fruition in the world, which is natural and reciprocal amity; which all the creatures maintain among themselves, and yet know not nor are able to consider, what and how great the force of that friendship is, for every one loves itself not out of hope of any reward and recompence to itself for it, but, because of the nearness and dearness it owes itself. Which if the same thing be not done in friendship, it is impossible to find a true friend.

He that loves you extremely, will hate you most deadly; therefore sober, moderate friendship is the best; and since friends must be had, if your happiness be to find good ones, beware you incur not that unhappi-

G　　　　nefs

nefs of changing them. Remember,
that he is in the beſt condition who
is beſt furniſhed with the beſt men
for his friends; neverthelefs, let no
obligation to them, make you dif-
penfe with your confcience or religion, have always a care not to truft
any thing to your moſt intimate pri-
vado, but what you cannot keep
from time· A fmall diſtaſte will dif-
cover thofe faults, which a heap of
years have covered. 'Twas *Bias*
his counfel that men ſhould fo love,
as if every day were a renewed en-
mity, and not to affeɛt repentance.

Let no man (which is the chief
law of friendſhip,) command any
thing of you, which is not lawful,
or which is not within your power;
nor do you ufe friends as men ufe
flowers, fmell to them as long as
freſh, and green, and fragrant, and
then lay them afide; for fo commonly friendſhips conciliated by intereſt or fancy, ufually terminate. Beware efpecially of mercenary love;
when your money fails, that leaves
you;

you, when true affection follows beyond the grave.

Your virtues will make and get you friends throughout the world. Love has arms which will join the distant corners of the universe; but the good offices you do at home, as they keep mens eyes upon them, and serve as well as remembrancers, will afford you a continued content.

Believe it, nothing will gain you so much respect, (the first and best ingredient to friendship) as your uprightness and sincerity; greatness was always suspicious, without any conspicuous proofs of a more than ordinary integrity, nor will true glory wait long on a false person; observance is her maid of honour, and what recommendation she gives must be founded on desert.

In a word, choose such friends as I have left you; they will be the more yours, because of your own affiance to them; and so you will have a double interest in them, your election and mine.

G 2   CHAP.

CHAP. V.

Of Travel.

THis is in some men a humour and curiosity only, in others wisdom and design, and accordingly they make their different returns, it hath been all along the practice of this nation, and with very good success: (to go to a foreign war is rather a transplantation than travel, passing only out of the bounds of one country, into the confinements and limits of another; so I reckon I have said nothing to you concerning this subject in my maxims of war;) and I cannot conceive any better divertisement (besides the advantage it will afford you) for your present condition.

Homer begins his *Odysseis* in the praise of *Ulysses*, with this title and character.—— *Qui mores hominum multorum vidit et urbes*, as the most apparent demonstration of his wisdom.

dom. Some men there are, that have seen more with their eye, than some ambitious princes did ever comprehend in their thoughts. 'Tis a pleasure and felicity when the mind embraces but a glancing thought of the beauteous fabrick of the universe, and is with a kind of delight transported to some peculiar part of it, whose felicity and pleasures, or wealth, have won upon its running fancy; if this be so in the imagination, what delight and fruition is there, in the corporal view, and passage, and abode in the most remarkable countries of the world? Men expect rich returns in *East-India* ships, and men that are far travellers, beget great expectation of their wealth; if they come home empty, they bankrupt their credit, and die in their country's debt; and that narrow dark prison of their pride, buries them in utter oblivion, who might have made the wide world their monument.

The story of the wandring *Jew*
was

was a pleasant fiction, the punishment consisted only in his not having a centre, and certainly he could as well want it as the rest of his nation. The moral would hint, what an improved man he must be who hath so often gone the circumference, cross'd the lines, and visited the most remote and abstruse corners of the world, seen so many varieties in nature and Providence, reconciled by the tract of time.

One journey will shew a man more than twenty descriptions, relations or maps; what a desolate life do tortoises live, who cannot be rid of their shells? No man can endure confinement; and he that hath lived lock'd up in one kingdom, is but a degree beyond a countryman, who was never out of the bounds of his parish. Nevertheless all men are not fit for travel; wise men are made better, and fools worse. This enquires after nothing but the guegaws, the antick-fashions, and gestures of other lands, and becomes

the

the fhame of all nations, by difgracing his own in carrying nothing of worth or efteem from thence, and by bringing cenfure and imputation upon foreign places where he converfed, by importing nothing but their vices.   They vent **abroad** their domeftick vices, and utter here, thofe beyond fea.

If you would advantage yourfelf by travel, you ought to note, and then comment upon your obfervations, remembring as well the bad to avoid it, as applying the good into ufe; without committing of thefe things to the pen, they will pafs from your memory without leaving any profitable refults behind them.

Let no hafte therefore hurry you through any confiderable or remarkable place, but ftay and view what is worthy in it, and be fure to regifter it with your pen, it will very much faften it in your memory; the charactering of a thought in paper, will fix it ready for your ufe; he that doth this, may when he pleafe re-

re-journey all his travels at home.

Solid persons are the best proficients by travel, they are not so prone to be inquinated by the drofs and feces of the vices, and taking vanities of foreign countries, being abler to compose themfelves to fuch manners, which may fooner facilitate their Inquifition.   Phance and outward freedom, and a feeming careleffnefs is the readiest way to get into strangers, and to learn from them.

Policy and negotiation I commend far before book-learning, though never fo deep and knowing. When you are abroad, the best way is to converfe with the best, and not to choofe by the eye but the ear, (which your own inexperience will foon warn you of) but follow report.

For the government, and things relating to the state, your advice and instruction is no where to be had but at court; for the trade, commerce and traffick, in great cities among merchants; for their religion and church-affairs, amongst the cler-

gy,

gy; but I rather choose the universities, where you may happily meet with an addition of the rest. For the laws customs and manners, the Lawyers, and for the country and rural knowledge, the husbandmen and such as we call the yeomanry.

All rarities are to be seen, and therefore I advise you not to travel without store of money to be ready at all occasions, especially antiquities, for these shew us the science and abilities of those times before us, (the moderns always preferring their arts and inventions to former ages) that by comparing of them with the present, we may be able to give a judgment, how the world thrives or goes less in all such learning.

Above all, think no travel too far nor discommodious to see and visit rare and eminent men; there is no monument like a virtuous learned person; living by him we shall be sure to be something the better, we shall find somewhat in him to in-

H flame

flame and excite our minds to strain
to the like pitch, and so extern them,
in a brave imitation of his excellent
qualities. To such men you must
carry yourself with all submiss reverence befitting the dignity of those
excellencies that are relucent in
them, and that awe you seem to
stand in, will soon invite his can-
dour to a free reception and near entertainment of you, for learned men
are rarely proud or stately.

Judgment is the only thing that is
necessary for a traveller, and therefore I approve not of your going a-
broad, nor permitting your children
if God shall send you any, till they
have grown to a good competency
of discretion, which yet I would
have seconded by the assistance of a
tutor, when it shall be any of your
inclinations this way. I pray God
bless you abroad, and return you as
an honour to your king, country
and friends.

CHAP.

C H A P. VI.

Of House-keeping and Hospitality.

THIs is a generofity very requi-
fite in noble perfons, and the
greateft demonftration they are fo :
'Tis as well refpected for the quality of it as the quantity, and according to the condition of every man ;
you may be as free in a moderate
entertainment as in all the excefles
and fuperfluities of your table, which
then becomes a fnare, where it
fhould be a kindnefs.

Neverthelefs, the greater extreme
is that of niggardlinefs ; and but a
little lefs than vilenefs or bafenefs, in
the eyes of your neighbours, which
will foon bring contempt and dif-
efteem upon you, which you muft
by all means (as reckoning it the
worft evil can befal noble perfons,)
avoid and decline. The *Englifh* are
fo careful of their honour in this

point,

point, that they do abridge themfelves of other grandezza's which
their eftates would afford them, as
coming to court, mafquing, &c. to
facrifice with the due rites to their
penates, their houfhold-gods, to
whom their anceftors had devoted
their prime fubftance, and which
the genius of their neighbouring people, as by a religious cuftom, expected from them.

So much was not required at the
hands of any *Scots* nobleman, as
from an efquire there of 2000 *l. per
annum;* the difference lies in the condition of our vaffals, and their tenants and neighbours, which being
perhaps now to be more affimilated,
both by fome ufe and underftanding
our nation hath of the *Englifh* Cuftoms, and the greater correfpon-
dency and mutual friendfhip, that is
likely to arife between them, (which
is now more advanced by the war,
than by the long projected union;)
I would advife you as far, and as
foon, as you are able, to comply
                                       with

with the *English* manners in this particular. It will beget a good re-spect; and favour purchased from hence is most durable.

To this purpose, keep constantly at home, without urgent and neces-sary occasions call you from thence. The entertainment your house will afford strangers, though it be never so ample and abundant, will want that condiment and sauce of hospi-tality, your own company. Men usually affect their landlord's com-pany, though they pay for it; much more will the honour of your pre-sence commend your frank and libe-ral treatments, to the gratitude of all persons who shall resort to your house and table.

Be not only courteous yourself to all comers, but see your servants be so too. Kind reception and admit-tance is as necessary before meat, as digestion afterwards; and he that would have thanks for his entertain-ment when it is past, must bespeak it before it begin at his board, that

his

his victuals and chear be but a rumination of his first kindnesses, and that his porch be as free as his hall.

Keep about you therefore no morose, cross-conditioned servants, and as near as you can retain men of a good aspect, and as far as you can be assured of them to be of fair and civil demeanour. Such will not only be an ornament and honour to you, but of much advantage; for as it will invite persons of quality and civility to you, which will be creditable for you, so will it shame and deter the ruder, and more ungoverned sort of people, who meeting with such dissonant humours, will soon abstain or soon be civilized.

Let not your entertainments be tedious, knowing that is not the way to keep them all along the year; and therefore substantial dishes must make up your bill of fare, instead of *French quelques choses.* Money and time is fruitlesly spent in those vanities, and are for no masculine contentment and palate; and if such be not your guests,

your

your expences will be *thrown away*, when others reckon them *laid out*.

Above all things avoid intemperance in drink. Luxury in feeding seldom carries men beyond their stomach and discretion, though never so many provocations be used to lure them on, but in the abundance of wine men are sottishly transported beyond themselves, and the excess in it, makes them the more covetous and raging after it, especially where they think or find they cannot be welcome, unless they comply with your humour, and can requite your charges no other ways, than by the loss of their sense and modesty.

I would have you therefore detest that barbarous *German* mode of drinking for victory, by a beastly subduing of those, whom you have invited, and humanely welcomed, and bid to your table. 'Tis one of the greatest vices our gentry hath brought from thence, amidst all those trophies which they deservedly gained there, and therefore the more

caution

caution is to be ufed, left it infinuate itfelf eafily by their converfe, whofe company you fhall do well always to efteem as an honour, but yet ufe your difcretion and my experience as an antidote againft that humour, which you may do plaufibly and indifcernibly enough.

Suffer no perfon to depart your houfe in difcontent, that fhall not by rudenefs or fome other unhofpitable way deferve your dif-refpect; on the other fide, permit no tumultuous diforderly perfons to ftay within your doors. Every ordinary man's houfe is his caftle; but a nobleman's is that and a palace both, where there is reverence due to you, as well as a bare power and command.

On publick anniverfary thankfgiving-days, you muft expend above your ordinary provifions. The folemnity due to thofe feftivals, takes its weight from the obfervation of the nobility, whofe magnificences at thofe times are the moft forcible impreffions to make the people remember

ber and call to mind, (which will alfo keep them in their duty,) the
mercies and favours of fuch days.
This will more especially concern
you, who by all means and ways
muft endeavour to reconcile yourfelf
to the government.

But be fureft, that the poor whofe
condition will not fuffer them within
your doors, may not be out of your
heart, but that a conftant care and
provifion be made for them from
whom I affure you, you fhall find
the greateft return and thanks, if not
by them, yet for them.

I   CHAP.

C H A P. VII.

*Of Tenants and other Concerns of E-
state.*

YOU will be at a loſs in this particular, by reaſon of the difficulties I ſhall leave upon my eſtate,
and the ſeveral claims made by pretended titles, beſides that which will
be eſcheated to the crown, it will
therefore require your utmoſt diligence and circumſpection, having ſo
many enemies about you.

I look upon your old demeans of
the family, as the moſt likely to continue in your poſſeſſion, and therefore you muſt retain and careſs with
all manifeſt demonſtrations of kindneſs, the preſent and ancient poſſeſ-
ſors and enjoyers of thoſe lands, who
by their long dependence on your
family, are ſo addicted to it, that
they will not deſire upon any ordinary conditions to be alienated from
you,

you, if you ſeem not to ſlight them
or your own intereſt.

It is utterly impoſſible you ſhould
be totally deprived of your inheri-
tance among them, ſo long as you
bear my name, nor do I know myſelf
every part of my eſtate there, ſo far
is it out of the reach of confiſcation:
many were the homages and ſervices
done me, which were without book.

For my novel acquiſts and pur-
chaſes, they have ſo much envy of
the ſtate already upon them, that I
would not adviſe you by ſtirring on
them to draw more upon you. your
old rents will be eſtate enough for
you, if you can ſecure them. I never
look'd upon any thing I had from
the eſtates of *Scotland*, other than as
a preſent ſatisfaction for what I had
expended; what it wants or exceeds
therein was never intended to be put
to your account.

'Tis no time now, nor is it your
intereſt to ſtand at that diſtance formerly maintained; many have been
the forfeitures of the *Scots* nobility,

yet I never knew any fo dangerous
as yours is like to prove, for I will
not diffemble that odium and envy
againft me, how juftly, I have laid
elfewhere.   So there lies upon you a
neceffity of counterwalking all ways
to your ruin   you muft move pity,
(and that I think no hard matter in
your cafe) and you will foon find
affection which will eafily be improved into truft and confidence, the
ready way to fecure your eftate.

If by fuch means, or any other
(as I do not, as I faid before, defpair of your total reftitution, if not
to your dignities and honour, yet to
your lands and revenues,) you fhall
be poffeft, remember you deal grate-
fully with fuch, as have dealt honeft-
ly and faithfully with you; and confider you may not ftrain things to
that heighth, which ufually great
men do in *Scotland*, for that the
wings of your greatnefs are clipped,
and cannot grow out again fudden
ly; and that your fafety now inftead of mightinefs, confifts altogether

ther in the love, and not in the fear of your tenants.

Redeem that hard cenfure laid upon me, of being a cruel rigid landlord, and ftrive to vanquifh thofe difficulties by a complacent carriage, which to my beft difpofed temper (as times were) proved infuperable.

Avoid as much as in you lieth all fuits and controverfies, fuch collifions will give light to difcoveries; fit down by any loffes or injuries, which you cannot remedy without publick trial, and give place to fuch violence as will overbear you.

Recollect firft your fcattered fortunes, and let a fedentary quiet life have confirmed you in the poffeffion of what you have, fo fhall you not be endangered (if then you be put to vindicate your right to what you enjoy) by that which you have not.

Contract your eftate into as few mens hands as poffible, change not thofe to whom you have let your lands formerly, or ufed or dealt with otherways; efpecially difplace not
fuch

such servants, who are acquainted
in the managing of it; for besides
the ease, you will find security in so
doing.

As I would not have you suffer
under that great depression of worth,
a base poverty, so neither would I
have you to be abused by the chargeable report of being very rich; to
avoid both, you must live in a free
and open way, neither like *Diogenes*
nor *Dives*: but yet the more men
are inquisitive after the secrets of
your estate, the greater will your
wisdom be, the closer to conceal it,
and that you may do without danger, for it is in your own defence.

Your estate will be safer however,
in the reputation of things past, (men
looking on my disposal and ordering
of it to be providential and munite
enough) than by your own wisdom
or any new present, foundation or
conveyance, which takes off a great
deal of envy from you.

Keep within the compass of what
fortune soever God shall bless you
with;

with; if you can be content you
fhall fruftrate the ruinous defigns of
your enemies againft you, who can
tell but all this may be for the better:
greater fhocks have been given to e-
ftates, which have but rivetted and
rooted them the fafter, inftead of o-
verturning them.

Whomfoever you intruft with the
ftewardfhip of your eftate, be fure
to truft yourfelf moft, and keep a
ftrict account of your disburfements
and receipts· befides, that it is a good
divertifement, you will find it very
profitable, and will contain and preferve your fervants in their duty,
and confequently in your favour.

Make not any neceffity by your
imprudence or prodigality, whereby
you muft be compelled to borrow
money by fecurity or mortgage, or
anticipate your revenues : the firft
will engage you to do the like cour-
tefies for your friend, and that's never without danger, and the other
two are bafely difhonourable, and
will foon bring contempt upon your
perfon,

person, and be a moth in your e-
state.

*Nullum numen abest, si sit pruden-
tia tecum.*

C H A P. VIII.

Of Study aud Exercise.

THE times succeeding I divine
to be very happy and peace-
able, and therefore a course of life
befitting the tranquillity of the age
you live in, will be to betake yourself to your studies.

You have read men a good part
of your life, and are pretty well
versed in that deep and profound
knowledge, that will be of use to you
in the bustles and encounters of the
world; you must also have some
provision to pass away the quiet and
blessed calm of life: but herein pray
observe these cautions.

1. That the study of vain things is a
   laborious idleness.
2. That there is no way which leads

ingc-

ingenuous fpirits more eafily, and
with more certain appearances of
honour and goodnefs, to delicacy,
foftnefs and unmanlinefs, than
learning and ftudy.

3. That to ftudy only to pafs away
time, is a moft inept curiofity,
and an unthrifting of time, and
very misbecoming active and
noble fpirits.

4. Though good letters be the beft
informers, yet company and con-
verfation are the beft directors for
a noble behaviour and deport-
ment.

You muft therefore fo order your
ftudies, that you make them fubfervient to the concerns of your honour, eftate, and intereft, and that
they entrench upon no time, which
fhould be employed about them.

Your vacant and fpare hours, you
cannot better afford to any thing
than to books, nay, there is a neceffity of making fuch leifure-time,
if the multiplicity of bufinefs prefs
too faft upon you, remembring that

K   of

of a great emperor, whose affairs
were not only urgent, but full of
trouble and care in a new attained
empire,——— *Nulla dies sine linea,* not
a day must pass without some im-
provement in your studies.

Your own choice and judgment
will best direct you what books you
shall read, and to what science you
shall chiefly apply yourself, though
I think it pedantical, and unworthy
and unhandsome for a nobleman or
person of honour to be affectedly excellent in any one; it seems as ridicu-
lous as *Nero's* mad ambition of being
counted the chief fidler and best
songster in the world.

History and the mathematicks, (I
may say) are the most advantageous
and proper studies for persons of
your quality, the other are fit for
schoolmen, and people that must
live by their learning; though a little
insight and taste of them, will be no
burden to you; your knowledge in
them, joined with your authority,
may be of good use to your coun-

try in awing of pragmatick profef-
fors, either of law or divinity.

I do not reckon the laws of the
kingdom any particular ftudy, for
they muft be your conftant practice,
your place may inftruct you in
them, as to the executory part of
them ; for the pleading part of them
that's below you.

Keep always an able fcholar for
the languages in your houfe, befides
your chaplain, who may be ready
at hand to read to you out of any
book, your fancy or judgment fhall
for the prefent pitch upon, you will
find him to be of great ufe and fervice to you, and give him falary accordingly.

Think no coft too much in pur-
chafing rare books, next to that of
acquiring good friends I look upon
this purchafe, but buy them not to
lay by, or to grace your library,
with the name of fuch a manufcript,
or fuch a fingular piece, but read,
revolve him, and lay him up in your

me-

memory where he will be far the better ornament.

Read seriously whatever is before you, and reduce and digest it to practice and observation, otherwise it will be *Sisyphus* his labour, to be always revolving sheets and books at every new occurrence which may require the oracle of your reading.

Trust not to your memory, but put all remarkable, notable things you shall meet with in your books *sub salva custodia* of pen and ink, but so alter the property by your own scholia and annotations on it, that your memory may speedily recur to the place it was committed to.

Review frequently such memorandums, and you will find you have made a signal progress and proficiency, in whatever sort of learning you studied.

After your studies give your mind some relaxation by generous exercises, but never use them after fulness, sleep, or oscitancy, for then they abate much of the recreation and

and delight they afford after intent-
ness of the mind on any business; o-
therwise it is but a continuation of
the dream in the stirring slumbers of
sport and play.

In the choice of your exercises,
affect none that are over-robust and
violent, that, instead of remitting, or
unbending the bow, will break it;
but let them be moderate, and with-
al virile and masculine, such as is ri-
ding the great horse, shooting at
marks out of cross-bows, calivers
or harquebuse. Tennis is not in
use among us, but only in our ca-
pital city, but in lieu of that, you
have that excellent recreation of
Golf-ball, than which truly I do
not know a better.

Do not make a toil of a pleasure,
by over-exercising your-self; play
not to wearisomness, which may
nauseate the recreation another
time to you. As near as you can,
play with companions your equals,
but if they are not at hand, pleasure will dispence with any play-
fel-

fellow, nor are you tied there to any strict rules of honour.

Let your exercises be designed to this end, to settle your mind, to beget you a stomach and appetite, and fit you for other succeeding business.

C H A P. IX.

Of Pleasure, Idleness, &c.

BY your recess from all publick business, you will be apt and prone to fall into some supiness and negligence, and indulge yourself in inordinate pleasures, if you keep not a strict guard over your inclination and bent that way, to which most men naturally are very subject.

Remember therefore, that great actions were never founded in vain delights, and nothing is less generous than pleasure, and nothing more corrupting the seeds of virtue, and that finally it ends in dislike and regret.

I acknowledge, that youth the
time

time of delight, is so transient and momentary, and man such a slave to himself, that notwithstanding all the troubles that befet him, he will find time, and space to bestow on his voluptuousness; but you have paft those heats of youth, and are arrived to a staid age, in which your debordery to vice, would be most shameful and odious.

But of all pleasures take heed of gaming, that's the vainest, and yet the most bewitching temptation. A vice which hath got footing amain among us, and alienated many fair lands and posseffions from ancient families; you may guess at its goodness by its extraction, born (as I may say) in a diffolute camp, where its first stake was the price of life, though contented here with livings and livelihoods. You have loffes more than enough already, do not therefore put any more to the injurious difposal of fortune, by dicing or carding, or any other game. That's the greatest sign of diffoluteness you

can

can give the world, which will pro-
claim you a vitious as well as bankrupt perfon.

Give not your mind to company
or drinking, thefe *Bacchanalia* are as
bad a game as the former. This will
prefently beftialize you, and take a-
way the fignature God hath ftamp'd
upon you. A drunkard! I cannot
name it without abhorrence, if it di-
veft you of your nature, it will not
leave you a fpark of honour, but
fink your eftate and all together, in
that deluge of ebriety. "Twas ob-
ferved by *Cato*, that none came fober
to the deftruction or overthrow of
that ftate but only *Cæfar;* moft certain it is, that none fhall ever be called to the maintaining of a ftate,
whofe debaucheries have made him
incapable of governing himfelf.

Avoid converfe with women of ill
report, that you be not fafcinated
by their beauty or arts, to the leffen
ing of that conjugal love you owe
your wife; men take it for a felicity
to enjoy the favour of the company
of

of fine women, but they reckon not to what dangers they oblige themselves, and what burdens they impose upon themselves to the secret ruin of their estates, for nothing is so chargeable as an imperious beauty.

Neither seek nor entertain pleasures when they present themselves in their gaudy bravery, but with a noble constancy keep your mind fast shut against their charms and allurements; but find some other diversion, the business whereof may send those vagrants packing. I do much commend hunting and hawking, and other field-pastime.

'Tis a dispute and an argument, whether to do ill, or to do nothing, *male agere aut nihil agere*, is the worst, and therefore in the next place shun idleness. The life of man resembles iron, which being wrought into instruments and used, becomes bright and shining, else unwrought the rust eats and consumes it; so is it with noble persons, if they exert themselves, and put forth their parts to

L the

the service of their country or in o-
ther honourable employments, they
become conspicuously glorious; better, industry should wear out and so
polish a man, than to ly by of no
use and service, and waste away in
sloth and idleness.

Nothing in the universe stands still;
the heavens and those orbes of light
are in perpetual motion, and though
the earth move not spherically, (as
Copernicus fancied) yet there is a continual *motus* in that too in her produ-
ctions: An idle man is a *mare mor-
tuum*, whose infectious company
spoils and ruins all that come near
his example. I do not admire to see
gentlemen given over to vitious cour-
ses of life, seeing they affect a lazy
greatness, without the props of employment to support it. 'Tis action
that keeps the soul sweet and sound.

I would have you keep no retain-
ers near you merely for show, but
only as many as you can well em-
ploy in their several offices; if you do,
you must expect no service nor atten-
dance,

dance, till they have first served their own pleasures, and besides you will have to answer for their lewdnesses.

You will have such a fragrancy and scent from any business you have been diligent in, as those that sit a-mongst perfumes and spices, shall when they are gone, have still a grateful odour with them.

If you grow not better by employing yourself, yet this benefit will surely accrue to you, that you both keep yourself from being worse, and shall not have time to entertain any suggestions of evil from without.

There is a kind of good angel waiting upon diligence, that ever carries a laurel in his hand to crown her; and fortune according to the ancients was not to be prayed unto, but with the hands in motion. How unworthy was that man of the world, or the enjoyments of it that never did ought, but only lived and died; and it is none of the ordinariest happiness, to be endued with a mind that loves noble and virtuous exercises.

L 2   Life

Life and honour confift both in
action, nor can they find a worfe
fepulchre than in the fluggard's field.
'Tis by fuch flothful men that the
monuments of their anceftors crumb-
ble into duft, and tomb-ftones are
obfolited by the fpeechlefs lives of
their fucceffors and children.

CHAP. X.

Confiderations of Life.

NO man is fo miferable as he
whofe life is hated by all, and
his death defired by as many.

I have known men that have fuf-
fered by fortune unexpectedly, and
having the calamity in their view,
have been fo far tranfported beyond
themfelves, that their rage and fury
even before juftice, hath proved their
fufficient defence.

Our trouble will never be at an
end, if we intereft ourfelves in other
mens bufineffes.

Great deliberation and flow refo-
lution

lution is required in the affairs of the world, for as in the trade of naviga-tion, the impetuousness of the sea is decried and charged with several ship-wrecks, so is it not otherwise in the affairs of men, where passion and unruly violence have overset many gallant designs and enterprises.

In matters in which you seem to have right on your side and justice also, a speedy dispatch is more need-ful than to languish through the de-lay of the remedy , on the other side, if you suspect the justice of your cause, the dispute and continuance of the difference is most profitable, and he-sitation is better than resolution, the disease better than the cure.

Be not dejected by knowing you are constrained to begin with small designs, for great affairs often begin from occasions far disjoined and re-mote from the end to which their undertakers aspired, for the begin-ning of designs reaches not so far as the issue.

Many small troubles are like letters

ters of a fmall print, they trouble and
offend our eyes, without the help of
the fpectacles of reafon and judgment;
but great adverfities we read prefent
ly and more eafily.

Sundry affections and paffions of
men may conceal themfelves, but
gladnefs is of the nature of fire,
which manifefts itfelf the more it is
ftifled and fmothered.

Follow not the fafhion of the
world, who, rather delight in praif-
ing of virtue than in imitating of it.

No life is fo full of content as to
live by one's felf, and meddle not
with other mens matters.

It is impoffible for any man to
live by fuch a rule of reafon, which
the frefh occurrences of things, time
and cuftome, may not innovate upon, and withall have informed him
fo much, that in what he pretended
to be well skill'd, he is a meer nov-
ice, and that which he efteemed
rare and excellent, to be unworthy
of his moft undervaluing confiderations.

Moft

Moft happy are thofe, who keeping a conftant tenour of life pafs through it without any danger, in the managery of bufinefs, or elfe live in a continual quiet and repofe in privacy and retirement.

It is a demonftration of greatnefs of fpirit and of prudence, to forget that which is loft and cannot be recovered, and to give way to thoughts defigning the amends otherways.

The body is pleafed and recreated only, during the time only of its pleafure, whereas the mind of man forefees future contentments and enjoyments, and fuffers not the memories of paft felicities to flip her repetition.

Youth giveth a tafte and indication of what may be expected from men; the reft of our time and feafons of our life, are appointed and defigned to reap, gather and receive the profits of what was fown in that age.

'Tis folly to complain of life, more to be troubled at the end of it, by the reafon we ought more to complain

plain of our birth, that made and produced us mortal, than of our death, which will render us immortal.

To be long or short-lived is no more than this, we come either sooner or later (no great choice) to our grave. He is very desirous of life, who is unwilling to die when all the world is weary of him.

'Tis not white or grey hairs, nor wrinkles in the face, beget a present respect for men, but a life honourably passed, confers glory and renown, and places the deserved wreath on their temples.

'Tis a strange infatuation in man, that he never takes thought how to live virtuously, but is very careful how to prolong his life from a loose principle, that it lies in the power of a man to live well, but it is out of his power to live long.

A life among roses, ends in a death among thorns and thistles, which proceeds always from those

intem-

intemperances and diforders our pleafures fway us to.

Life is a continual longing, and a continual naufeating, and all human reafon, judgment, and art cannot by any ways remedy it, and who would be a flave to fuch viciffitudes?

They are very miferable who have nothing but a heap of years to prove they have lived long, but infinitely unhappy are they who furvive their credit and reputation.

There is no better defence againft the injuries of fortune and vexation of life, than death.

Make your eftate the bound of your defires, and not your defires the limits of your eftate, but the beft and equaleft boundary to both is death.

M   MAXIMS

MAXIMS

OF

STATE,

BY THE

Marquis of ARGYLE.

CHAP. I.

The Prince.

THERE is nothing in the world which wins more upon the affections of men, or makes a prince more reverenced and defired than clemency, it is alfo neceffary, that he keep himfelf in a conftant tenour, duly tempering that gravity (which majefty requires) with debonarity and fweetnefs; that all acceffes to him be eafy, that he carefs and efteem, and give kind reception to all perfons of worth, difcountenancing the vitious, and cafting out flatterers, liars, and fuch like, of whom no fervice may be expected.

'Tis the excellence of a prince to ufe his clemency in pardoning fuch as offend, and for which offence any reafonable, equitable excufe may be alledged, as alfo in abating the rigour of the law to fuch, who tranfgrefs not out of cuftom, and are o-
ther-

therwife perfons of repute and of virtue, and whofe faults are not a-trocious, for if he exercife his clemency other than fo, without thefe confiderations, he will be rather cruel, and unjuft, than merciful; whereas counterpoifing it with e-quity, his juftice is noway interefled againft it, being reduced and applied to its true caufe.

It is lefs difhonourable for a prince to be vanquifh'd by arms, than by munificence and bounty.

That revenge which a prince takes from his fenfe of a perfonal injury is always efteem'd rigorous and too fevere though never fo juft.

'Tis fatal to all princes, who have fwayed fceptres in their minority, to be embroiled with troubles and feditions in the beginnings of their reign, and tormented by fome of their fubjects defirous of novelty; but when they have attained to age and the full exercife of their power, they have quickly learned to chaftife and punifh thofe infolencies and out-

rages

rages committed againſt them in their youth.

Ordinarily princes do not uſe to love ſuch, who are acquainted, ſee and reprehend their vices; neverthelefs, they cannot ſo carry them, but that notice will be taken; nor avoid the cenſure which is become the town-talk.

Neighbour princes muſt not go ſee or frequent campaigns of war, left in ſo doing, they draw upon themſelves hatred and envy.

A prince muſt be conſtant in retaining his good friends and ſervants, and entertain no ſiniſter opinion of them, without great, juſt, and apparent cauſe; to govern himſelf by his own counſel, and to be maſter of himſelf, that is, of his affections and opinions, by reducing them to ſage and mature advice.

The prince who is too cruel in the puniſhment of crimes, whether ſuppoſed or true, gives occaſion of cenſure, that it is out of covetouſneſs after the condemned's goods, and

and that he is fwayed more by ava-
rice than juftice.

Princes muft have a care they fuffer not any fubject, to grow near
them in fuch grandeur and puiffance,
which, their boldnefs may foon make
redoubtable to them; but muft cut
them in the root: for if that greatnefs once be radicated, it is almoft
impoffible to pull it up without the
abfolute ruin of thofe who attempt
it, as of late experience *Wallenftein*
Duke of *Friefland.*

It hath often happened that the
memory of a good prince deceafed,
hath been of good ftead to his vitious fucceffors, degenerating from his
virtues, and hath made their government tolerable.

A prince ought to be vigilant and
careful, that he be not furprized by
the ordinary importunity of craving
courtiers, in pardoning faults which
he ought to have punifhed.

Princes muft not make ufe of (like
private men) artifices and flights,
which

which will foon hazard their perfons and eftates.

Couragious princes are moft commonly fubject to love *Mars* and *Venus*, which are oftimes link'd together.

Kings muft fometimes vifit the remoteft parts of their country, that their fubjects may fee by their care of them, that they are truly the paftors of the people.

The children of kings are to be taught to fpeak low and gravely.

It is neceffary that a great monarch fhould be univerfally knowing. Private men for their direction, content themfelves with one fingle virtue, but a fovereign muft have all; for who hath more need of prudence and wifdom, than he who deliberates, and refolves fuch great and important affairs? who ought to be more juft, than he who governs the laws? who ought to be more referved, than he to whom all is permitted? and who hath more need of courage and valour, than he who protects and defends all?

Truth never or feldom approaches the ears of princes without a difguife, or blemifh'd by the injury and cunning of thofe, who would indirectly gain the favour of the prince without deferving it.

A prince ought to take counfel when it pleafes himfelf, and not at the will of another; if he be not fufficient of himfelf, he will hardly be well advifed if he be not committed to the conduct of one particular perfon, who is folely and entirely to govern him, and whatever good fhall be effected by his counfels ought to be afcribed to the prudence of the prince, rather than his counfellors.

The beft counfel that can be given to princes, who are well advanced in years and in extreme old age, and who muft leave unexperienced raw fucceffors, is to treat rather of peace and alliances with their neighbours, than to enterprife a war.

A king is obliged as diligently and

carefully to keep the goods of his crown, as a tutor those of his pupil.

A prince must be punctual in his religion, for nothing so sadly presages his ruin, as his negligence in that, and therefore his most lively thoughts must be intent on it, and in serving God without hypocrisy.

It much imports a prince, to preserve union and friendship with his brothers, as being the dearest part of himself, and as ready to his assistance, as his own eyes, his hands, and his feet.

Princes must beware of attempting what's above their strength, or to enterprise any thing in which they are not sure to come off with honour.

Kingdoms, treasures, the robe of purple, the diadem, are not such splendid ornaments of a prince, as virtue and wisdom; for a prince that knows himself to be but a man will never be proud.

Those princes then begin to lose their estates, when they begin to

break

break the ancient laws, manners and cuftoms, under which their fubjects have long lived; for princes muft have as much regard to the fafety of their fubjects, (which confifts in the protection of the laws) as of their lives.

A prince newly come to the crown, muft efpecially avoid giving any occafion to his fubjects, to wifh and figh for the government of his predeceffor, as the people of *Rome* did under *Tiberius*, after *Auguftus Cæfar*.

When princes fend ambaffadors, they muft chufe fuch whofe manners and qualities are fuitable and agreeable to the court whither they are fent.

A good prince does not only do good to the good by making them better, but alfo to the bad by reftraining them from being worfe, and the felicity of fubjects, is the true glory of kings.

Princes are miftaken that think to reign over men, without permitting God to rule over them.

The

The requeft of a prince is equal to a commandment.

Princes fometimes difgrace their favourites for their good, and reftore them again for their hurt.

A prince who truly is and effectually appears to be religious, is always feared and reverenced by his fubjects, who will never rebel or revolt from him, believing that he is under the particular protection of God.

Offences which princes take are like fixed pillars, but their love like the fpokes in a running wheel.

Princes beftow offices, favourites give admiffion, nature good extraction, parents patrimony, and merits give honour, but wifdom and difcretion come from God alone, and are not in man's difpofing.

Kings have divers forts of thunder as well as *Jupiter*, that which tears and rends all that refift it in folid bodies; and that which paffes the foft and pliable.

The fcience which we learn by
books,

books, is water out of a ciftern, that which we gain by experience is living water, and in its fpring; fo though among fcholaftick men we find couragious and refined polite fpirits, yet princes take not ufually fuch as they intend for their fervice from the fchools though they be knowing and able perfons, for 'tis bufinefs and action that ftrengthens the brain, while contemplation weakneth it.

'Tis difhonourable for a great prince or monarch to defend and maintain with his quill, what his predeceffors have acquefted with their lance.

A prince that would get much, muft pardon much; though 'tis a maxim among grandees, efpecially fuch as are raifed from obfcurity, that though they be mortal, yet the indignities done them are immortal.

'Tis folly to folicite tedioufly great men, for a thing which cannot be obtained.

The good words of a prince, ac-
com-

companied with promises, are most forcible and powerful engines.

'Twas a precept of the emperor *Charles* V. to his son king *Philip* II. to exercise himself always in some virtue befitting and convenient for a king, to the end that holding his subjects in admiration of his actions, no time should be given their thoughts to entertain other affections.

He must never see the picture of fear any where, but on the shoulders and backs of his enemies.

It is not only a sign of modesty and clemency, but also of a superlative courage, when kings take no notice of ungrateful mens speeches.

Nothing can please a good king so much as concord among his subjects, whereas that makes a tyrant to fear them.

A prince must by all means prevent, (slighting not the smallest things) and obviate factions and conspiracies, for as the loudest storms and tempests, are caused by secret exhalations and insensible vapours.

so

fo feditions and civil wars, begin often from light occafions, and which no man would think could come to fuch an iffue.

The retinue and train of a prince, let it be never fo retrench'd and ordered, is always very troublefome to the places through which they pafs.

'Tis a true foundation and principal maxim of ftate, to have an eye to the growing greatnefs of a neighbour prince, and to have always a jealous fear of his power; this makes the friendfhip between them more firm and durable; for when they have reafon alike to dread one another, either of them will but coldly attempt a breach.

The will of a prince is to be executed, not interpreted.

Princes commonly pay flatterers in their own coin; for they diffemble the vices of the princes, and they diffemble the lies of the flatterers.

At the death of a prince, 'tis difcretion to feem neither forrowful nor glad.

A

A prince cannot be faid to be potent, who is not ftrong at fea, and cannot join maritime to his land-forces.

When mean princes pafs the limits of mediocrity, they are near paft the bounds of fecurity.

It is neceffary, that a prince defer nothing to the deliberation of his council of eftate, which hath not firft paft the counfel of his confcience.

It is not good to frequent the prefence of a prince whom you have offended; he was well advifed, who having provoked his fovereign, protefted, that he would never fee his face more but in picture.

They muft be ftrong and downright blows, that can batter down a puiffant crown.

The treaties between princes fhould refemble *Drufus* his building or *templum fidei*, which were conftantly clear, nothing of obfcurity, nothing feigned, and without any coverture.

This fhould be a leffon and rule for all princes, that the faults which

O   they

they suffer and tolerate in their subjects, are as so many burdens laid upon their own shoulder, and of which
they must give account to the majesty
of him to whom they as much as
other men are subjected.

Great princes ordinarily endeavour
to bring petty ones into their snares,
or to do their affairs at their expence,
they embark themselves in their
quarrels, and forget and leave them
out in the accommodation of them,
and under colour of defence and
assistance keep those places for their
own, which were put into their
hands for gage and caution.

Nothing renders a prince more
contemptible then niggardliness, for
'tis odious in all men, but especially
in them, who as they are placed in
an ampler and more opulent fortune
than other men, ought to be more
liberal and free from base parsimony
and covetousness.

The greatness of that prince is
sure and stable, which his subjects
know to be as much for them, as
above them.   A

A prince mounted on high will have high afpiring thoughts, 'Twas great *Alexander's* fpeech, that it was proper to good princes to do well, and to hear ill.

It were very expedient that a prince who inherits his realm, fhould inherit alfo the minifters of ftate, to aid him in the government, thofe that have been ufed to the managery of affairs, are of more knowledge than thofe that newly enter upon the adminiftration, who being ignorant of the caufes and firft defigns, either fpoil all prefently, or fo turn the courfe of the policy of the ftate, that confufion follows.

CHAP. II.

Of Courage.

IT hath been the glory of *Scotland,* that fhe hath fent forth as many famous warriours into the world as any nation whatfoever; of later years more efpcially, in the *Swedifh*

and

and imperial war under the great captain *Guftavus Adolphus,* as alfo in *Rufsia, Poland, Prufs,* and moft parts of *Europe.* Moft of thofe hero's were perfons of very good extraction and noble families, neither fhould I miflike it if any of you, except my fon *Lorn* fhould undertake an honourable expedition. His neceffitudes and affairs at home, will require more of the gown than the fword: for truly I do count glory fo atchieved, to be the more folid and durable, as having that ftiff compofition of the fteel in it, whereas the other comes by the plume, and is apter to take wing and be gone. Befides, our name challengeth you into the field, our anceftors were eminent for the military way, and therefore I fhall here lay you down fome maxims of approved ufe, taken from the moft experienced captains, and fome of my own obfervations.

Courage is an innate moral virtue placed in the mind, whereby it o-verlooks and contemns all difficulties

and

and dangers ſtanding in its way, to the attainment of glory; 'Tis the ſublimeſt of all other vertues, by means whereof they do exert themſelves in their greateſt ſtrength and beauty.

Courage is an expoſing of the body to the utmoſt hazards and dangers, and venturing through the moſt invincible hardſhips, for of how little concern is that man that cannot elevate himſelf above common diſcourſe?

The laurels and the coronets are not half ſo glorious, as the flaſhings of the ſword, the exploſion of the muſquet, and thoſe wounds which men fairly gain in the ſervice of their princes.

In a generous ſoul age enfeebles not courage.

Nothing more touches a valiant man to the quick, than to ſee the event not anſwer expectation, and that fortune gives law to vertue.

Matters of danger, not deſpair, are the true objects of valour; every virtue is tied to rules, and bounded with limits, not to be tranſgreſſed; the extremes

tremes alter all goodneſs if they be pitch'd upon. Courage loſeth its merited honour, if willfullneſs and overguided petulancy overbear it; a well grounded reaſon, without prejudice to a mans honour may juſtly countermand a raſh and unconſiderate reſolution.

Nothing in the world can truly be ſaid to be great, if that heart be not ſo, that deſpiſeth great things.

'Tis natutal for brave ſpirits, not to hold their tongues in the very face of danger, or in fear of ſervitude.

A great heart neglects ceremonies, for by how much the more generous it is, the leſs it regards the luſtre and ſplendor of exteriour things, eſteeming itſelf its own theatre.

Bees turn not drones, nor courages ever abate or degenerate.

By the way, I obſerve that none have ever arrived to an eminent grandeur, but who began very young.

There's no place where a man cannot enter into which a ſun-beam can penetrate; nothing so constant and so firm, but what a firmer courage can beat and shake it.

Noble souls are ashamed to see that thing which they cannot remedy.

They are to be esteemed valiant and magnanimous, who repell injuries, and not those that do them.

'Tis better to trust in valour, than in policy.

As the light is open to all eyes, so nothing can be shut against valour and magnanimity.

C H A P. III.

Of War.

WAR is either foreign or intestine, civil war always hath been, and for ever will be the most destructive and ruinous, more pernicious than all the other evils of famine and pestilence, which angry heaven can inflict upon cities or kingdoms designed for utter ruin; so passionately
ly

ly *Livy* expresses its unnatural fury.

Men enterprise a war, either relying on the strength and assistance of God, or else upon humane power, when men therefore are provided with neither of these, when trial is made, captivity, or some such misfortune is the conclusion, nor are the best armed both these ways, sure of the victory.

In a war that's just, (for I allow no other,) the ancient men ought to counsel, and the young to execute.

To do nothing out of course or without orders in war, is of very ill consequence; for while time is spent in waiting for them, *occasio rei gerendæ perditur,* many noble designs are lost; the reason is, because directions being to be had at a great distance, they usually come too late for execution; and 'tis the nature of war to produce every moment some unlook'd for difficulties.

'Tis better to attain if possible by peace the half of our demands, than

by

by war the whole, for a war is sooner kindled than extinguished.

War proceeds from the ambition and malice of men, but the success of it depends on the good will of God.

In domestick broils, the greatest victory is never to be victorious, rather to level demands by a peace than mount to them by a conquest.

By prevention, revulsion and diversion, oftentimes men have gained by the war, when nothing but confidence makes men losers.

A civil war is nothing but the flux and reflux of conquests and losses.

In war 'tis punishable with death to hold a place, which is not tenible by the military rules, else every hen-roost would make an army stay in its march.

In a fair war, a man may see from whom to guard himself, but in a slubbered peace, a man knows not in whom to trust.

When the heart of the soldiery fails, all commands are to no pur-

P   pose;

pofe; for fear cafts a mift over their memory, and the practice without courage is to no purpofe in times of neceffity.

The events of war are uncertain, fmall fkirmifhes end in a fet battle, which is fought oftentimes more out of eagernefs and heat of blood, than prudence.

Mifchief in the beginning of a civil war, though not well fupported at firft, grows higher like the luxuriant branches of a fruit-bearing tree, but if a good patriot like a gardner put in his pruning hook, the fuckers are foon cut off, and the ftock remains entire.

All manner of ftratagems are lawful in war, though not practicable in ftate-policy. The fight and fhew of new engines of war to the befieged hath been the only caufe of their furrender.

Money is the finew of the war, but without the fomentation of a large treafure will foon fhrink.

C H A P.

CHAP. IV.

Of Command.

WHO commands in any place, ought to put a fentinel upon his mouth, that nothing unadvifed flip from him; and bear fuch a countenance, that the fair out-fide may varnifh his feverity within. Men that are cholerick, though they may be apt for learning, yet are not fit to command.

Negligence is no point of excufe in a governor of a ftrong important place, for if a truce or (may be) a peace be concluded on, yet he ought to confider that he is not concerned in that peace, having in his cuftody that which is well worth the breaking of it.

Never think of governing others, till you have the government of yourfelf.

To command and obey that which is commanded, is the moft exquifite art; thefe two keep a city free from

fedition,

fedition, and preferve concord.

Diverfity of commands is dange-rous, for that the execution of them cannot be femblable, for when one fees his counfel or command is not followed, he grows regardlefs, and may be out of emulation is the caufe of hindring the others (though bet-ter) counfel to take effect.

It is convenient and neceffary, that thofe who command, keep a diftance from their inferiors, to be-get in them a reverence and awe to-wards them.

Merit is the only lawful afcent to places of truft, and he who thinks to climb without it, may at the return mifs the fteps, and precipitate himfelf.

C H A P. V.

Of Victory.

BY the bloody fword victory is obtained in an hour, but to keep up the reputation of it is mat-ter of trouble through the whole life.

There

There is no victory so glorious, as that which is got with the least effusion of blood on the conquerors side, and which conserves the honour and justice of his cause.

He only accounts himself vanquished, who is satisfied that neither stratagem, nor treachery, nor fortune, had any thing to do in his overthrow, but only clear valour in a noble and just war.

He that hath vanquished his enemies, may make no difficulty of subduing himself.

It is of no great moment, with what provisions or furnitures of men and arms a victory is atchieved, for that conqueror is more renowned, who by a handful of men attain'd it, being succoured and seconded by his valour alone.

When the original is lost, men must be content with the copy; and to take all in good part what the conqueror pleaseth without replying a word.

Seldom men know how to make advan-

advantage of their victories, with that of the *Carthaginian* general,——
Vincere scis Hannibal, uti victoria nescis.

Anger and victory omit no kind of revenge.

The vanquished have this solace in their overthrow when it is done by the arms and by the valour and conduct of a noble person.

That's the best and compleatest victory, which is without destruction.

C H A P. VI.

Of Fortune.

FORTUNE hath more force than reason in the decision of war, yet it can do little harm to us, so long as it takes not away our honour.

It is not enough to know how to remove the machine of a great design, unless we know also when to let it alone, and to comply with time and necessity.

'Tis God that dissipates the devices of the nations, and brings to nothing the designs of the people; the king is not saved by the strength of his arms, nor shall the mighty man escape by his great power.

As the understanding of a man is not always in vigour, nor the body in health, so many times men enterprizing great things, fall and hazard themselves, lose their hopes and designs, and sometimes their lives.

Idleness and luxury have subdued more arms, than ever were vanquished by plain force: what a fatal intemperance and sloth was that of the *Carthaginians* after the battle at *Cannæ* to suffer the *Romans* to make head again?

Mature deliberation ought ever to be used; but when arms are to determine, speedy execution is best: because no delay in that enterprise is fit, which cannot be commended before it be ended, and victory has determined it.

Soldiers must be encouraged in all
fortunes

fortunes to ftand refolved; that which was the enemies good luck to-day, to-morrow may be theirs, they muft not be daunted with any paft mifadventure, ever attending a time and opportunity of revenge, which commonly cometh to pafs where mens minds are united; for common danger muft be repelled with union and concord.

Some conquefts are of fuch quality, as albeit a victorious captain merit triumphal honour, yet a modeft refufal becomes his greateft glory; as fome noble *Romans* did out of bravery of mind before the emperors, and fome for the envy of it, did forbear it afterwards.

To enter into needlefs dangers was ever accounted madnefs, yet in times of extreme peril and apparent diftrefs, bold and hazardous attempts are the greateft fecurity, and are ufually feconded with good events.

To conclude, *Melior tutiorque certa pax quam fperata victoria.*

Mifcel-

GREAT perfonages may preferve their honour without taint or crime, but not free from fufpicion; the firft is in their own power, the fecond depends on the ill-will of others.

Toleration is the caufe of many evils, and renders difeafes or diftempers in the ftate, more ftrong and powerful than any remedies.

It moft commonly proves true, that a council compofed of diverfe nations, (fuch as was projected by *Cromwell* in *England*, during his ufurpation in conftituting a reprefentative of three kingdoms in one body,) are of different judgments and tempers, though never fo well pack'd together: But yet that is a far worfe diverfity, which proceeds from the variety of particular paffions, that corrupt the fountain and fource from whence the advice and counfel of publick affairs is to be drawn.

'Tis a received maxim among confpirators, not to have any thing pafs

Q

be-

between them in writing, but orally and by word of mouth.

Men would seem to be very jealous of their honour, when for words spoken in prejudice or diminution of it, they commence suits and processes against the speakers of them, but there is nothing so below a generous spirit, and which argues more weakness of mind, than that they cannot contemn words that are vain and uttered in haste. I can set my approbation to this, that I never knew any man that got advantage by so doing.

For men who have high thoughts and low fortunes, 'tis better to live privately and meanly in a village, than beggarly and disrespectedly at court.

Men of virtue and honour steer a course contrary to that of the world, as do the planets above.

Nothing is so sociable or dissociable as man, the one is caused by nature, the other by vice.

The pleasure or grief of present things takes up the room in our thoughts of what is past, or what is

to

to come, fo infirm is the moft fubli-
mate human reafon fubjected to the
attempts of fortune.

Prudence ought to begin all affairs, for that repentance is to no
purpofe in the end, wifdom rather
prepares than repairs. Wife men
walk not always in the fame way,
nor keep always the fame pace, they
advife according to the occurrence of
affairs, and vary according to the
alterations of time and intereft.

It belongs to prudent men to fore-
fee that adverfity and misfortunes
come not before their time, (then
all the wifdom of the world cannot
ftay them) and it appertains to valiant men, when they are come, to
bear them courageoufly.

Prudence without virtue, is rather fubtilty and malice, yea is quite
another thing than prudence.

Nothing ought to be done violently or precipitantly in reformation,
you muft wind up the ftrings gently
to make them tunable, the mufick
founds a great deal fweeter, when
they

they are loofer, than when ftraighter wound.

He is fure not to fail, who has virtue for his guide, and fortune for his companion ; but he that travels fuch a way, muft begin young, elfe he will come late to his journey's end.

'Tis certain, that he who deviates from truth, is in the ready way to all forts of mifchief, and it hath often been feen, that fuch who have laid their hopes in lying and diffembling to others, have deceived themfelves, to their own ruin.

The moft abfolute perfection of men cannot be refembled better than to a pomegranate, which is never without fome rotten kernels.

Nothing more grieves fubjects to pay fubfidies and taxes, than when they fee their money wafted or ill employed, who otherwife where they pay a penny would willingly give a crown, for they take notice that when once the door is opened to im pofitions, under pretence of continuing but fo long time, it is feldom

shut

shut again, this is true in all tyrannical or absolute governments.

Nothing appeases or quells a sedition sooner than the presence of the prince, nor ought he for any fear or cause whatsoever absent or hide himself, our late troubles speak this too evidently.

It is an ill practice, that they who have been the greatest sticklers in state-troubles and commotions, should be the greatest gainers by the accommodation of them.

Seditions whose originals cannot be traced, are always the most dangerous.

The due correction of a mutinous people brought again to obedience, ought to be regulated by examples and means accommodated to the time, and disposition and humour of the country; the laws must give place to policy.

Always observe, that a paltry ordinary fellow in a great sedition is commonly the chief, and such an one is harder to be spoken or treated with, than any prince or general.   In

In a civil war betwixt subjects of the same prince, misery follows the vanquished, cruelty and impiety, haunts the conquerors, ruin and destruction both the one and the other.

That people can never be at ease, whose prince is indebted.

Let this be a lesson to the people to contain themselves within the bounds of their duty, for by engaging in the quarrels of the great ones, they are commonly plunged in the mire, while their leaders trample over them to security.

Nothing is impossible, or unfeasible for an enslaved people to do against tyrants and usurpers.

He that keeps himself strictly to the observation of the divine laws, cannot err in the human, and he that is a good servant of God, will never be an ill subject to his prince.

Such a prince, and such a people, I pray God for ever to maintain and continue in these nations.

F I N I S.

Ingram Content Group UK Ltd.
Milton Keynes UK
UKHW050732220623
423745UK00024B/284